# One Wide Expanse
*Michael Longley*

*A collaboration between the*
THE IRELAND CHAIR OF POETRY
*and*

UNIVERSITY COLLEGE DUBLIN PRESS
*Preas Choláiste Ollscoile Bhaile Átha Cliath*
2015

First published 2015

UNIVERSITY COLLEGE DUBLIN PRESS

UCD Humanities Institute

Belfield

Dublin 4

Ireland

www.ucdpress.ie

ISBN 978-1-906359-89-8

ISSN 2009-8065

CIP data available from the British Library

The right of Michael Longley to be identified as
the author of this work has been asserted by him

Typeset in Adobe Kepler
Text design and setting by Lyn Davies Design
Printed in England on acid-free paper
by Antony Rowe, Chippenham, Wiltshire

# Contents

# FOREWORD

It might seem at times that the power of the imaginative gesture has been lost or, at least, overlooked in the complex and busy world in which we live. The ceaseless interconnectedness and endless instant communication can appear to preclude reflection.

But it is not so. Imagination surrounds us and lives within us – all of us have inner lives. And public policy and public institutions also retain the capacity for imaginative action.

Thus, it was a wonderfully creative response to the award to Seamus Heaney of the Nobel Prize for Literature that the Ireland Chair of Poetry was established in 1998. Five institutions from both jurisdictions on the island of Ireland came together to support the initiative. The Irish Arts Council/An Chomhairle Ealaíon, the Arts Council of Northern Ireland, Queen's University Belfast, Trinity College Dublin and University College Dublin set themselves the task of bringing this new role into existence, have sustained it ever since, and are committed to its long-term future as a central part of the literary life of the island. What this Chair of Poetry will achieve will be greater than what might have been conceived by those who brought it into being.

John Henry Newman said that writers were 'the spokesmen and prophets of the human family'. By this he did not mean that they were or should be the daily chroniclers of the times in which they live. It was, rather, recognising that writers and artists can at once reflect and shape the nature of their society. Poets have a powerful capacity to offer a prophetic voice that can elevate human experience and enhance our understanding of ourselves. Seamus Heaney captured the possibility well when he said 'if poetry and the arts can do anything, they can fortify your inner life – your inwardness'.

One of the essential features of the Ireland Chair of Poetry is that it has a public role – deliberately so. Each holder of the Chair spends a term in each of the universities across the three-year period of office. That allows an active engagement with the life of the university community and, crucially, with its students. The Professor also gives a major public lecture in each of the three years.

From the beginning it was the clear intention that these lectures be published. The lectures of the first three Professors, John Montague, Nuala Ní Dhomhnaill and Paul Durcan, were published a number of years ago as one volume. In the past year, the Trustees took the decision that the lectures of each Professor should be published as soon as possible after the period of office. This set of lectures by Michael Longley is, therefore, the first in what will be a continuing series. It will be followed later this year by the lectures of Harry Clifton and next year by those of the current Professor, Paula Meehan, when her term in office will have ended.

The wisdom and worth of the decision to create the Ireland Chair of Poetry has been reflected in the distinction of those who have held the position and in the many and varied ways in which they have given expression to its potential and brought poetry to the people. It is a pleasure to give them thanks. As it is, also, to acknowledge and applaud the Arts Councils and the Universities for their sustained support for and commitment to the founding vision.

Finally, it is proper to remember with special thanks and appreciation the deep personal interest that Seamus Heaney had in this project and his dedication as a Trustee from the inception of the Ireland Chair of Poetry to the time of his death.

BOB COLLINS
*Chair of the Board of Trustees, Ireland Chair of Poetry*
February 2015

# A Jovial Hullabaloo

The great American poet Wallace Stevens begins his poem 'A High-Toned Old Christian Woman' with this line: 'Poetry is the supreme fiction, madame.' In the course of a complex poem he weighs in the scales religious belief and the life of the imagination. Although he clearly prefers the latter, he seems to compromise by suggesting that both end up creating the same thing: 'A jovial hullabaloo among the spheres.'

> Poetry is the supreme fiction, madame.
> Take the moral law and make a nave of it
> And from the nave build haunted heaven. Thus,
> The conscience is converted into palms,
> Like windy citherns hankering for hymns.
> We agree in principle. That's clear. But take
> The opposing law and make a peristyle,
> And from the peristyle project a masque
> Beyond the planets. Thus, our bawdiness,
> Unpurged by epitaph, indulged at last,
> Is equally converted into palms,
> Squiggling like saxophones. And palm for palm,
> Madame, we are where we began. Allow,
> Therefore, that in the planetary scene
> Your disaffected flagellants, well-stuffed,
> Smacking their muzzy bellies in parade,
> Proud of such novelties of the sublime,
> Such tink and tank and tunk-a-tunk-tunk,

May, merely may, madame, whip from themselves
A jovial hullabaloo among the spheres.
This will make widows wince. But fictive things
Wink as they will. Wink most when widows wince.

This evening I shall be talking about how I discovered poetry as a reader and writer of it. I shall be celebrating some of the poems and poets who have mattered to me. *A Jovial Hullabaloo* will be an autobiography in poetry.

At Malone Public Elementary School in Balmoral Avenue in South Belfast we ten-year-olds recited aloud, as a sort of ragged chorus, David's great lamentation over Saul and Jonathan. I relished the rolling rhythms generated by the strange words, and didn't worry too much about the meaning.

> Saul and Jonathan were lovely and pleasant in their lives,
> And in their death they were not divided:
> They were swifter than eagles,
> They were stronger than lions.
> Ye daughters of Israel, weep over Saul,
> Who clothed you in scarlet, with other delights,
> Who put on ornaments of gold upon your apparel.
> How are the mighty fallen in the midst of the battle!
>
> [2 Samuel 1:23-5]

The New English Bible of 1970 flattens the rhythms in an attempt to be clearer. In the King James Bible (as we've heard) 'Saul and Jonathan were lovely and pleasant in their lives, /And in their death they were not divided'. In the New English Bible this becomes: 'Delightful and dearly loved were Saul and Jonathan; / in life, in death, they were not parted.' Though not completely dire, this is neither poetry nor prose. It is verbal polystyrene. It is forgettable. The translators of the New English Bible tried to be contemporary, but their version just ended up being temporary. The King James Bible was written to last. It has inspired many poets. It was composed to be memorable. In poetry the meaning cannot be detached from the melody. In Malone Public Elementary School at least one ten-year old's mind was saturated with beautiful words.

In Form III at 'Inst' (the Royal Belfast Academical Institution) when I was fourteen, I was mesmerised by Keats's 'La Belle Dame sans Merci' and by Walter de la Mare's 'The Listeners'. De la Mare bridges the worlds of nursery rhyme and modern poetry:

'Is there anybody there?' said the Traveller,
    Knocking on the moonlit door;
And his horse in the silence champed the grasses
    Of the forest's ferny floor:
And a bird flew up out of the turret,
    Above the Traveller's head:
And he smote upon the door a second time;
    'Is there anybody there?' he said.

That year I chose for my Third Form English Prize the *Collected Poems* of W. B. Yeats, published by Macmillan with a creamy dust-jacket and maroon boards. The choice alarmed my family.

Joe Cowan, a dapper little Englishman with a pert moustache, taught me English in Sixth Form. It was Joe who awakened in me (and, a year or two later, in Derek Mahon) a passion for poetry. There was little or no Irish literature on the syllabus in those days, so Joe xeroxed for us poems by living Irish writers – Patrick Kavanagh, Louis MacNeice, W. R. Rodgers. He would hand around the sheets. 'Read that one aloud for us, Longley,' he'd say. I'd read, and then he'd ask: 'Is the man a poet?' Embarrassed mumbles. 'Is the man a poet? I should say so! I should say so!' And he'd chortle and slap his thigh.

When I was sixteen I first seriously tried to write poetry – a combination of hormonal commotion and aesthetic awakening. But it wasn't until I went to Trinity College Dublin that poetry grew into an obsession. My career as a Classics student was already in serious decline. Perhaps I was looking for something else at which to shine.

At school I had immersed myself in classical music, and explored in a daze of pleasure the beautiful big art books in the library. Now it was poetry, or the idea of poetry, that took me over completely. I filled notebooks with formless outpourings, writing several bad poems a day. The first piece I ever submitted for publication was a crazy prose poem, like a mad dog's howl, which I dropped into the post-box of the undergraduate literary magazine *Icarus*. I wasn't expecting it to disappear forever – but it did, mercifully.

Eventually, in the March 1960 issue of *Icarus* two of my juvenilia were published. After forty-eight years the thrill reverberates still. One of the poems was called 'Marigolds':

She gave him marigolds
the colour of autumn
to keep in his cold room,
and the late light of autumn
gilded all their moments.

That Easter I went home to Belfast. My father discovered 'Marigolds'. 'Michael, it's not worth the paper it's written on,' he said. Over the years I have written obsessively about my father as a boy-soldier in the Great War. Forty years after 'Marigolds' and perhaps in response to his dismissal, I wrote these four lines:

He would have been a hundred today, my father,
So I write to him in the trenches and describe
How he lifts with tongs from the brazier an ember
And in its glow reads my words and sets them aside.

['Anniversary']

At Trinity Brendan Kennelly, a fellow student already publishing poems, was generous in his praise and encouraged me very early on. He encompassed everything I had been missing. Coming from Belfast, with my English parents and Protestant schooling, I had never encountered anyone quite like him. He was culturally astonishing. Decades later, in a poem called 'The Factory', I evoke the enduring impression he made on me:

> Already the tubby, rollicking, broken Christ
> Talking too much, drowning me in his hurlygush
> Which makes the sound water makes over stones.

Just as I was jostling to lay claim to the title 'college poet', Derek Mahon breezed in from Belfast – a year or two my junior but fully fledged, it seemed – brilliant and self-confident. I was flummoxed. This was one of the best things ever to happen to me. We became good friends. As I have said elsewhere, we inhaled poetry with our Sweet Afton cigarettes – Hardy and Auden and MacNeice. For years the closing lines of MacNeice's 'Mayfly' have been watchwords of mine:

> The show will soon shut down, its gay-rags gone,
> But when this summer is over let us die together,
> I want always to be near your breasts.

It pleased us that Presbyterian Ulster could produce an exotic like the clergyman-poet W. R. Rodgers:

> Dance, Mary Magdalene, dance, dance and sing,
> For unto you is born
> This day a King. 'Lady,' said He,
> 'To you who relent
> I bring back the petticoat and the bottle of scent.'

['Lent']

We had those lines by heart, and still do. We loved Dylan Thomas's fruity recordings. (All the poets of my generation were intoxicated by Dylan Thomas. I could prove this by showing you some very embarrassing juvenilia, my own especially!)

We revered the D. H. Lawrence of the animal poems and the love poems and the great death psalms, and Robert Graves, the muse-poet supreme:

> She tells her love while half asleep,
>   In the dark hours,
>     With half-words whispered low:
> As Earth stirs in her winter sleep
>   And puts out grass and flowers
>     Despite the snow,
>     Despite the falling snow.

['She Tells Her Love While Half Asleep']

For my twenty-first birthday a friend gave me Kavanagh's *Come Dance with Kitty Stobling*. I have never thought in Irish dynastic terms and I don't see myself or my poetic colleagues in some kind of Irish succession. I dislike literary ancestor worship. But if I *had* to choose two Irish poetic uncles, they would be Louis MacNeice and Patrick Kavanagh – the Kavanagh who wrote this immaculate lyric:

> Consider the grass growing
> As it grew last year and the year before,
> Cool about the ankles like summer rivers
> When we walked on a May evening through the meadows
> To watch the mare that was going to foal.

['Consider the Grass Growing']

As I was beginning to write in the late 1950s three new English poets published astonishing first collections. I was excited by their largeness of vision and by the way they renovated the language. In 'Wedding-Wind' from Philip Larkin's *The Less Deceived* a young bride soliloquises:

> Can it be borne, this bodying-forth by wind
> Of joy my actions turn on, like a thread
> Carrying beads? Shall I be let to sleep
> Now this perpetual morning shares my bed?

Can even death dry up
These new delighted lakes, conclude
Our kneeling as cattle by all-generous waters?

*Lupercal* was in fact Ted Hughes's second collection. Of its several spell-binding animal poems, perhaps my favourite is 'The Bull Moses', at once earthy and cosmic:

Each dusk the farmer led him
Down to the pond to drink and smell the air,
And he took no pace but the farmer
Led him to take it, as if he knew nothing
Of the ages and continents of his fathers,
Shut, while he wombed, to a dark shed
And steps between his door and the duckpond;
The weight of the sun and the moon and the world hammered
To a ring of brass through his nostrils.

The third of these collections, *For the Unfallen* by Geoffrey Hill, begins with 'Genesis', which he composed when he was still in his teens. He seems, in part, to be writing about the genesis of poetry itself:

Against the burly air I strode
Crying the miracles of God.

And first I brought the sea to bear
Upon the dead weight of the land;
And the waves flourished at my prayer,
The rivers spawned their sand.

And where the streams were salt and full
The tough pig-headed salmon strove,
Ramming the ebb, in the tide's pull,
To reach the steady hills above.

The coincidence of these three poets of genius marks a pinnacle in the history of English poetry. It was a good time to be an apprentice.

At Trinity we bought the early collections of Thomas Kinsella, John Montague and Richard Murphy as they came out from the Dolmen Press. We took in Baudelaire and Brecht. Thanks to the Penguin Modern European Poets series you could for a few shillings give yourself a rudimentary education in European modernism: the great Russians – Ahkmatova, Pasternak, Mandelstam, Tsvetayeva – four poets sustaining one another in the sub-zero chill of Stalin's Russia, a sodality of imaginations; and Apollinaire and Ungaretti – especially, so far as I was concerned, the poems they wrote as soldiers in the Great War. We looked to the precocious Rimbaud, and were only half joking when we said that we would consider ourselves failures if we hadn't published our first slim volumes by our early twenties.

I'll now read the first two stanzas of Derek Mahon's 'In Belfast' (which he has re-christened 'Spring in Belfast'):

Walking among my own this windy morning
In a tide of sunlight between shower and shower,
I resume my old conspiracy with the wet
Stone and the unwieldy images of the squinting heart.
Once more, as before, I remember not to forget.

There is a perverse pride in being on the side
Of the fallen angels and refusing to get up.
We could *all* be saved by keeping an eye on the hill
At the top of every street, for there it is,
Eternally, if irrelevantly, visible –

When Mahon's poem was published, the Professor of English Philip Edwards wrote it out on the blackboard for his students. I felt envious when I heard that. In this poem and in other early pieces like 'Subsidy Bungalows' and 'Glengormley' Mahon shows that the shipyards and the working-class estates of Belfast are just as much a part of the Irish landscape as the Donegal hills or the wilds of Mayo.

In my Trinity rooms we listened again and again to the Harvard Poetry Library recordings of American poets – Robert Frost reading 'After Apple-Picking', the lilt of E. E. Cummings, and Wallace Stevens (still my favourite reader of poetry) reciting 'The Idea of Order at Key West':

> Oh! blessed rage for order, pale Ramon,
> The maker's rage to order words of the sea,
> Words of the fragrant portals, dimly-starred,
> And of ourselves and of our origins,
> In ghostlier demarcations, keener sounds.

We gutted the work of Robert Lowell, Theodore Roethke, Hart Crane. 'In Memoriam', the first of my elegies for my father, was sparked off by Lowell's autobiographical sequence 'Life Studies'. And I am still excited by his early masterpiece 'The Quaker Graveyard in Nantucket':

> You could cut the brackish winds with a knife
> Here in Nantucket, and cast up the time
> When the Lord God formed man from the sea's slime
> And breathed into his face the breath of life,
> And blue-lung'd combers lumbered to the kill.
> The Lord survives the rainbow of His will.

My most ambitious early poem 'The Hebrides' (which I wrote towards the end of 1964) takes its bearings from 'The Quaker Graveyard' and mixes equal measures of George Herbert and Hart Crane.

In some of his most brilliant poems Herbert creates a repeated pattern of lines of different lengths. In his poem 'Peace', for instance, the metrical pattern consists of lines of ten, four, eight, six, ten and four syllables. Painfully difficult they may be, but these complicated stanzaic shapes with fixed rhyme schemes generate jazzy syncopations and blue notes. Here is a stanza from George Herbert's 'The Flower', one of the loveliest poems in the language:

And now in age I bud again,
After so many deaths I live and write;
I once more smell the dew and rain,
And relish versing: O, my onely Light,
It cannot be
That I am he
On whom Thy tempests fell all night.

This is lyrical writing of an aching, almost unbearable refinement. Can poetry get any closer to the grain of the language? In my inner ear such quietude attracted the tidal surge of some lines by Hart Crane – from the second poem in his great sequence 'Voyages'. Like 'The Flower', 'Voyages II' is a poem that has just about everything:

Bind us in time, O Seasons clear, and awe.
O minstrel galleons of Carib fire,
Bequeath us to no earthly shore until
Is answered in the vortex of our grave
The seal's wide spindrift gaze toward paradise.

George Herbert and Hart Crane might seem odd bedfellows, the Anglican vicar communing with his God and the suicidal lover of sailors cruising the waterfront, but they seem to get along fine in my poem 'The Hebrides':

· Here, at the edge of my experience,
Another tide
Along the broken shore extends
A lifetime's wrack and ruin –
No flotsam I may beachcomb now can hide
That water line.

\* \* \*

Beyond the lobster pots where plankton spreads
Porpoises turn.
Seals slip over the cockle beds.
Undertow dishevels
Seaweed in the shallows – and I discern
My sea levels.

'The Hebrides' is dedicated to Eavan Boland. Derek Mahon introduced me to her in 1964. She held forth about poetry with extraordinary flair and authority. She challenged me. Indeed, she intimidated me. I have never been much good in intellectual debate. I think Boland noticed how few opinions I have. In answer to her questioning I wrote 'The Hebrides', and dedicated it to her. I remember reciting it to her in a Dublin pub – by heart. I meant it to be both gift and confrontation. The subtext was: 'This is as brilliant as I shall ever be.' I hope that our minds meet on the Hebrides.

In the anthology *Watching the River Flow* I write about the cultural apartheid that operated between the two Dublin universities:

> Extraordinarily, there was next to no literary interchange between TCD and UCD (let alone Cork where Eiléan Ní Chuilleanáin was a student). If we Trinity poets were learning from each other, how much more skilled and versed we might have become had we jousted with the likes of Michael Hartnett, Eamonn Grennan and, later, Paul Durcan who were inhabiting a parallel universe in Earlsfort Terrace.

Poetry did bring us all together in the end, but long after our college days.

Towards the end of my Dublin sojourn I shared with Mahon a malodorous basement flat in Merrion Square. I describe the Beckettian scene in my memoir *Tuppenny Stung*, and I record that: 'These were fulfilling rather than happy times. Our friendship and our abilities were often stretched as far as they could go.' By this time Mahon had published some extraordinarily accomplished poems. I owed much to his brilliant practice, his verve and edginess. But I myself had been travelling quickly, without taking a breath, from my rather wan juvenilia to the aspiring shapes of my first reasonable poems.

I was punch-drunk when I arrived back in Belfast in 1963. I wasn't ready to take in another authentic new voice. So at first I didn't accurately register Seamus Heaney's early poems. They sound so natural it is easy to miss their originality – poems such as 'Digging' and 'Death of a Naturalist', which were dissected at sessions of the now over-mythologised Belfast Group. Initially I had no desire to attend The Group. Prompted, I now know, by Heaney, Philip Hobsbaum the prime mover invited my fiancée and me along.

I began to enjoy what was for me as a lapsed classicist a new experience – practical criticism. In *Tuppenny Stung* I refer to 'the kitchen heat of the discussions', and suggest that friendship 'remains for me the most important legacy of The Group. The poetry would have happened anyway. But Hobsaum brought some of us together and generated an atmosphere of controversy and excitement.' After one fierce disagreement (not, I might add, at a Group meeting) I walked backwards out of a crowded room, shouting at Hobsbaum and, from a parcel under my arm, dropping sticks of rhubarb on to the floor.

Perhaps Hobsbaum's hot advocacy of Heaney's work got in the way of my own appreciation of it – but only initially. Images such as the frogs at the flax dam 'Poised like mud grenades, their blunt heads farting' or the butcher-shop turkey invoked as 'A skin bag plumped with inky putty' or the clothes of the milk-churners 'spattered / with flabby milk' – such images have been lodged in my synapses ever since those early days. It is as though the particulars of life on an Ulster farm were inventing a language for themselves – a dialect that our senses seem always to have known. Take, for instance, 'Cow in Calf':

Slapping her out of the byre is like slapping
a great bag of seed. My hand
tingled as if strapped, but I had to
hit her again and again and
heard the blows plump like a depth-charge
far in her gut.

Depth-charges, indeed. Awakenings. In a barn on a hot summer's day something almost religious can happen, something both visionary and matter-of-fact:

> A scythe's edge, a clean spade, a pitch-fork's prongs:
> Slowly bright objects formed when you went in.
>
> ['The Barn']

Was I bit high-handed with my new friend? Heaney held his ground in any case, and stood up to Mahon and me when we were being bossy one evening. I can still hear him saying: 'I'd love to write like you boys but I've got to go on my own and write my kind of poems.' Wonderful. Nevertheless, I sense that his move from the early paragraph-like poems to the sculpted quatrains of 'Follower' and 'Personal Helicon' owes something to what Mahon and I were attempting. In 'Personal Helicon', his beautiful lyric about wells and boyhood and imagination, the poet sinks an artesian well into the reader's subconscious and 'set[s] the darkness echoing':

> One, in a brickyard, with a rotted board top.
> I savoured the rich crash when a bucket
> Plummeted down at the end of a rope.
> So deep you saw no reflection in it.
>
> A shallow one under a dry stone ditch
> Fructified like any aquarium.
> When you dragged out long roots from the soft mulch
> A white face hovered over the bottom.

The poetry we wrote then, indeed much of the poetry that has since emerged from the North of Ireland, has been dismissed by unsympathetic critics under the heading 'the well-made poem'. This is meant as a pejorative term, but it is in fact tautological. Any poem that works – be it expansive in Walt Whitman's style or tightly packed à la Emily Dickinson – is bound to be well made. You might as well talk about a 'well-made flower', or a 'well-made snowflake'.

Yeats said that he wrote in form because if he didn't he wouldn't know when to stop. Like Samuel Beckett I prefer the word 'shape' to 'form'. At Trinity during a course on Aristotle's *Poetics* our Greek professor W. B. Stanford told us to come back the following week with our own definitions of poetry. Mine was: 'If prose is a river, then poetry's a fountain.' I still feel that's pretty good because it suggests that 'form' (or 'shape') is releasing rather than constraining. The fountain is shapely and at the same time free-flowing. The American poet Stanley Kunitz puts the case for form perfectly: 'A badly made thing falls apart. It takes only a few years for most of the energy to leak out of a defective work of art. To put it simply, conservation of energy is the function of form.'

I introduced Mahon to Heaney, and Heaney introduced me to James Simmons. Simmons melded the energies of popular culture with his own lyric gifts. The best of his work – poems like 'Stephano Remembers' and 'From the Irish', songs like 'The Silent Marriage' and 'Claudy' – will live on. He founded *The Honest Ulsterman* in 1968 and, after a while, handed the editorship over to Michael Foley and Frank Ormsby. Foley (who favoured the more demotic Simmons) christened Mahon and Heaney and me The Tight-Assed Trio. (It might be worth recalling that *The Honest Ulsterman* School of Literary Criticism went in for fine shades of discrimination: there were three types of bad poetry: Shite, Dogs' Shite and Mad Dogs' Shite.)

In the early 1970s, at the beginning of my stint as Literature Officer with the Arts Council of Northern Ireland, Ormsby and Foley called to discuss their grant with me. I had just published in the *New Statesman* two verse letters – one addressed to Mahon, the other to Heaney. I had submitted to *The Honest Ulsterman* a third verse letter (addressed to James Simmons). I foolishly presumed they'd be delighted to print it. The supplicant editors told me: 'Those two poems in the *New Statesman* were bad enough; but with this third one to Jimmy Simmons you've disappeared up your own arse completely!'

The Tight-Assed Trio was kept on its toes. In the late 1960s Heaney showed me some poems by a schoolboy called Paul Muldoon. A little later in 1968 I met Muldoon after a poetry reading in Armagh. Eventually he joined the BBC as a producer, and I embarked on another exacting friendship. No sooner had the Tight-Assed Trio begun to work out how things might be done, than a brilliant new generation came along hell bent on deconstructing our best efforts – Paul Muldoon, Medbh McGuckian, Ciaran Carson, Frank Ormsby, Tom Paulin.

I am now grateful for that challenge and for the stimulation of the next group of Northern poets: Peter McDonald, Sinead Morrissey, Leontia Flynn, Nick Laird, Alan Gillis. (The work of an even younger cluster of live wires was recently showcased in the locally published anthology *Incertus*.) So, there has been little or no opportunity for self-congratulation or self-importance. This has been a lucky chance for me, a gift of life. Who was it who suggested that self-importance inscribes its own gravestone?

Over the years my poetry has become simpler. When I revise I seek to simplify and clarify. An ideal poem, for me, would be 'Tall Nettles' by Edward Thomas. A poet I first read at Trinity, he has by now moved to the centre of my imaginative life:

Tall nettles cover up, as they have done
These many springs, the rusty harrow, the plough
Long worn out, and the roller made of stone:
Only the elm butt tops the nettles now.

This corner of the farmyard I like most:
As well as any bloom upon a flower
I like the dust on the nettles, never lost
Except to prove the sweetness of a shower.

Like George Herbert, Edward Thomas possesses the poetic equivalent of perfect pitch. I have revisited 'Tall Nettles' hundreds of times. Like all true poems it is always brand new – 'Worn new / Again and again', as Thomas himself says in his poem 'Words'. Regarding subject-matter he made a statement which I consider crucial: 'Anything however small may make a poem. Nothing however great is certain to.'

Edward Thomas was killed by a shell-blast at the Battle of Arras in April 1917. Other geniuses died in the Great War: Wilfred Owen, Isaac Rosenberg, Charles Sorley. I revere these lost soldier-poets as well as those who survived the slaughter – Siegfried Sassoon, Robert Graves, Edmund Blunden, Ivor Gurney. It is wrong to confine such writers to the dubiously simplified category of War Poet. When I read a poem like Owen's 'Insensibility' or Rosenberg's 'Dead Man's Dump' –

None saw their spirits' shadow shake the grass,
Or stood aside for the half used life to pass
Out of those doomed nostrils and the doomed mouth

– I picture the young Sophocles and the young Aeschylus trudging under the weight of their kitbags through the terrible mud.

In terms of scale there is no way we can compare the Troubles with the industrialised devastation of the Great War. But I am reminded of the War Poets when I consider my contemporaries and our apprenticeships in a damaged society. Owen's desperate desire to befriend and impress Sassoon feels familiar to me, as does the poetic transformation that Sassoon's (and Graves's) encouragement brought about in Owen's writing. After the War, Graves and Sassoon befriended and helped Edmund Blunden; and then, in his turn, Blunden edited collections of Wilfred Owen's and Ivor Gurney's poems. As they tried to make sense of the nightmare of the trenches the War Poets were listening to each other.

In the early 1970s poets here were as dumbfounded as most people by the ferocity of the violence. Seamus Heaney has written of the 'search for images and symbols adequate to our predicament.' And in 1971, in a survey of the arts in Ulster called *Causeway*, I suggested that the poet 'would be inhuman if he did not respond to tragic events in his own community and a poor artist if he did not seek to endorse that response imaginatively...'. I added that the poet 'needs time in which to allow the raw material of experience to settle to an imaginative depth ... He is not some sort of super-journalist commenting with unfaltering spontaneity on events immediately after they have happened. Rather, as Wilfred Owen stated, it is the poet's duty to warn ...'

In such monumental poems as 'Easter 1916', 'Meditations in Time of Civil War', 'Nineteen Hundred and Nineteen', W. B. Yeats loomed large, an inescapable exemplar. More than any other poet he helped us to find our way through the minefield. Like Wilfred Owen in the trenches, Yeats demonstrated that the complex, intense lyric is capable of encompassing extreme experience:

> Now days are dragon-ridden, the nightmare
> Rides upon sleep: a drunken soldiery
> Can leave the mother, murdered at her door,
> To crawl in her own blood, and go scot-free ...
>
> ['Nineteen Hundred and Nineteen']

We did not write in Yeats's shadow, as some would have it, but in the lighthouse beam of his huge accomplishment.

To be a poet is to be alive to both precursors and contemporaries. As regards my contemporaries from Northern Ireland, this may have been so in a further sense as poets here, with their different backgrounds and perspectives, reacted to the Troubles. Poems are aware of each other. No poem is a solo flight. In his wonderful lyric 'The Friendship of Young Poets', the Scottish poet Douglas Dunn conjures up an ideal scene:

> There is a boat on the river now, and
> Two young men, one rowing, one reading aloud.
> Their shirt sleeves fill with wind, and from the oars
> Drop scales of perfect river like melting glass.

The American poet and critic Randall Jarrell famously tells us: 'A good poet is someone who manages, in a lifetime of standing out in thunderstorms, to be struck by lightning five or six times; a dozen or two dozen times and he is great.' And Rilke says somewhere: 'You ought to wait and gather sense and sweetness for a whole lifetime ... and then, at the very end, you might perhaps be able to write ten good lines.' The enterprise often feels like a long wait for something that does not necessarily happen. In 'How Poetry Comes to Me' the American Gary Snyder writes a poem about writing a poem:

It comes blundering over the
Boulders at night, it stays
Frightened outside the
Range of my campfire
I go to meet it at the
Edge of the light

It is mysterious why some people write good poems and then stop; and mysterious why others persist. I think being a poet is different from being a writer. Some poets are writers as well but they are usually protecting a core. Poetry can't be created to order. You can't write your way out of a poetic block. I have no idea where poetry comes from, or where it goes when it disappears. Silence is part of the enterprise.

For me Keith Douglas is a pivotal and still underestimated figure in modern poetry. As an undergraduate he was encouraged by Edmund Blunden. In 1944 he died on the Normandy beaches. He was only twenty-four. When he was barely twenty, Keith Douglas had this to say:

Poetry is like a man, whom thinking you know all his movements and appearance you will presently come upon in such a posture that for a moment you can hardly believe it a position of the limbs you know. So thinking you have set bounds to the nature of poetry, you will soon discover something outside your bounds which they should evidently contain.

Moving one's 'bounds' as a writer of poetry involves, invariably, the renewal of rhythms. To quote Yeats again: 'As I altered my syntax, I altered my intellect.'

I myself am drawn more and more to poets who do things that I can't do. I have been enjoying the New York school of poets who came into prominence mid-century, at the same time as the Abstract Expressionists: in particular Frank O'Hara, James Schuyler and Kenneth Koch (whose reading here in Belfast I introduced a few years ago. There's an elegy for Koch in *Snow Water*). Frank O'Hara finds hilarious ways to be serious. He invites us, as Yeats puts it, to get down off our stilts. In his cod manifesto, 'Personism', he discusses poetic form:

> As for measure and other technical apparatus, that's just common sense: if you're going to buy a pair of pants you want them to be tight enough so everyone will want to go to bed with you.

(So, perhaps, after all, the improvisatory Frank O'Hara belongs with the Tight-Assed Trio!)

How does a poem like James Schuyler's 'Sleep' work? It was written in a mental hospital. It mentions St Valentine's Day. The poet's eye wanders around the institution and records seemingly random particulars in a mode that manages to be both casual and ceremonious:

> The friends who come to see you
> And the friends who don't.
> The weather in the window.
> A pierced ear.
> The mounting tension and the spasm.
> A paper-lace doily on a small plate.
> Tangerines.
> A day in February: heart-
> Shaped cookies on St Valentine's.
> Like Christopher, a discarded saint.
> A tough woman with black hair.
> 'I got to set my wig straight.'
> A gold and silver day begins to wane.
> A crescent moon.
> Ice on the window.
> Give my love to, oh, anybody.

I don't know many lines as heartbreaking as that last line: 'Give my love to, oh, anybody.'

One thing I have learnt from the New York poets is that good art is often nobly dishevelled. Throughout my fifty years of writing, when the creative buzz comes on, I have felt sizeable, capacious like Walt Whitman; but when I've written the poem and typed it out I realise that I am still Emily Dickinson – the pernickety Emily who, when asked for her opinion of *Leaves of Grass*, said of Whitman, 'I never read his book – but was told that he was disgraceful.'

I have worshipped Emily Dickinson since my Trinity days (there's a poem about her in my first collection). I read Whitman of course, but the penny has only recently dropped. How could I have managed without him for so long? How can there be 'a jovial hullabaloo' without Walt Whitman? He will be the last poet I'll quote from this evening – from his sequence 'Sands at Seventy'. 'To Get the Final Lilt of Songs' is a short poem about old age and about reading and writing poetry:

> To get the final lilt of songs,
> To penetrate the inmost lore of poets – to know the mighty ones,
> Job, Homer, Eschylus, Dante, Shakespeare, Tennyson, Emerson;
> To diagnose the shifting-delicate tints of love and pride and doubt
>    – to truly understand,
> To encompass these, the last keen faculty and entrance-price,
> Old age, and what it brings from all its past experiences.

For six months in 1993 I was Writer-in-Residence (Writer Fellow) at my old university, Trinity College. From a large number of submitted portfolios I selected for my creative writing workshop a small group of undergraduates. I'm still proud of my choices. Some of those students have gone on to make names for themselves: Caitriona O'Reilly, David Wheatley, Justin Quinn, Sinead Morrissey. (The novelist Claire Kilroy was also a key member of my group.) I have kept in touch with all of them. Sinead Morrissey's achievements and reputation grow apace.

She now teaches creative writing here at Queen's. As I begin my professorial sojourn I look to her (and to another brilliant young poet Leontia Flynn) for guidance and inspiration.

Now, as Ireland Professor of Poetry, I feel that I have come full circle. As I start to meet students in the three universities, I am reminded of something the American poet Donald Hall says about his life in poetry. Hall describes the effort to write poetry as having 'conversations with the dead great ones and with the living young.'

*A transcript of a lecture given in the Great Hall, Queen's University, Belfast, on St Valentine's Night 2008.*

IN MEMORIAM

Joe Cowan
Alec Reid

# One Wide Expanse
*a Return to the Classics*

Much have I travell'd in the realms of gold,
  And many goodly states and kingdoms seen;
  Round many western islands have I been
Which bards in fealty to Apollo hold.
Oft of one wide expanse had I been told
  That deep-brow'd Homer ruled as his demesne;
  Yet did I never breathe its pure serene
Till I heard Chapman speak out loud and bold:
Then felt I like some watcher of the skies
  When a new planet swims into his ken;
Or like stout Cortez when with eagle eyes
  He star'd at the Pacific – and all his men
Look'd at each other with a wild surmise –
  Silent upon a peak in Darien.

I

That, of course, is John Keats's great sonnet 'On First Looking into Chapman's Homer'. The 'wide expanse' is open to everyone. Keats, after all, didn't know Greek: he had just discovered 'the realms of gold' in the majestic translations of George Chapman, the Renaissance English poet. Today several translations of the *Iliad* and the *Odyssey* are available in paperback (including Chapman's). Over the last five decades the literatures of Greece and Rome have again become an abundant source for poets writing in English.

For instance, since the 1960s Irish writers have found in Greek tragedy ways of dealing with the Troubles. One thinks of Tom Paulin's *Riot Act* which portrayed the individual – Antigone – confronting authority. Seamus Heaney also turned to Sophocles's *Antigone* (which he called *The Burial at Thebes*) and to *Philoctetes* (which became *The Cure at Troy* with its celebrated chorus:

> History says, *Don't hope*
> *On this side of the grave.*
> But then, once in a lifetime
> The longed-for tidal wave
> Of justice can rise up,
> And hope and history rhyme.)

Derek Mahon produced a witty *Bacchae* and in *Oedipus* a sombre conflation of Sophocles's Oedipus plays. In terms of theatrical excitement Brendan Kennelly's *The Trojan Women* has been for me the most thrilling adaptation. Tom Murphy, Aidan Mathews, Frank McGuinness, Brian Friel, Marina Carr and Colin Teevan make it a long list of contemporary Irish writers indebted to the Classics – lining up behind Synge and Yeats who called the Greek and Latin authors 'the builders of my soul' – and, of course, not forgetting Louis MacNeice, the brilliance of whose version of the *Agamemnon* must have something to do with his being, out of them all, the only fully fledged classical scholar. (The other plays I've mentioned are, broadly speaking, translations of translations.)

The last few years have seen a steady flow of books about the classical world. Clearly publishers believe that classical scholarship sells. In the *Observer* last September Tom Holland wrote: 'People are not stupid – they know when they are missing out on something interesting and important. If the education system fails to give it to them, then it can hardly be surprising that they will look for it elsewhere, in works of popular history, perhaps, and in other media as well.' Feature films and TV dramas come to mind, Hollywood blockbusters and computer games. In his forthcoming edited collection of essays *Living Classics* Stephen Harrison discusses the 'paradox that classical texts have achieved a high profile in contemporary literature at a time when fewer people than ever can read these works in the original languages.' Despite this trend, and after something of a lull, an increasing number of students now want to study Latin and Greek. In 2000, there were a mere one-hundred-and-fifty non-selective state schools in England offering Latin; now there are more than five hundred. The British government is in fact putting both languages *back* onto the curriculum. But there is now a shortage of qualified teachers. Seven years ago I (and others) tried to persuade Queen's University to keep Latin and Greek 'on the curriculum' when it had decided to close down the Classics Department. I shall let my letter to the newspapers speak for itself:

> As an honorary graduate of Queen's University, I am angered and bewildered by the Academic Council's decision to close down the Classics Department.
>
> With respect to politics, philosophy, language, poetry, drama, architecture, mathematics, the sciences, sport we are all of us three quarters Greek and Roman, whether or not we realise it.
>
> The so-called academic planners who would close down Latin and Greek are wiping out a crucial part of the map by which we know ourselves and find our way.
>
> Have the barbarians arrived? Yes. But worse they are in charge.
>
> I pray that the university will think again.

So far, it hasn't shown any sign of thinking again.

Our Professor of Greek at Trinity College, W. B. Stanford, used to say 'chalepa ta kala' – 'the beautiful things are difficult'. Reading the Classics could be tough going – even tougher was trying to compose prose and, sometimes, *verse* in Greek and Latin. I hope that my own poetry has been strengthened by these rigours. Much contemporary writing sounds to my ears syntactically flabby, linguistically impoverished. In losing touch with Latin (and Greek) it has lost its backbone.

II

I have been haunted by Homer for fifty years. Now I would like to say something about what 'that wide expanse' has meant to me. I treasure my battered copy of Stanford's edition of the *Odyssey*. Charlie Fay, our Classics master at the Royal Belfast Academical Institution (Inst for short), encouraged us to write the date at the end of each book of the *Odyssey* when we had finished reading it. I completed my first, Book X, just before Christmas 1956. There in the pernickety hand of the classical annotator is the date: 17. xii. 56. I was just seventeen, but like some elderly scholar I filled the margins with notes about the unseen digamma, the gnomic aorist, epexegesis, sociative datives and other technicalities that now mean little or nothing to me. During each class we would slowly translate ten or twenty lines, and then read the Greek aloud. Somehow the Homeric sunshine broke through all that cloudy donkeywork. I loved the sound of the Greek, the bumpy hexameters, the clash of the broad vowels, the way lips and tongue are vigorously exercised, hammer and tongs. And of course I adored the stories.

Fay was an intimidating and sometimes cruel figure. He had me studying the *Agamemnon* when I was only sixteen. He used to knit in class – serious knitting – socks and gloves. Once, when I was half-way through a chorus in the *Agamemnon* – gasping to find the main verb – he shouted at me: 'Quiet, scum, I'm just turning the heel!' Many years later, when I was well into my fifties, I spotted him in the interval crowd at the Lyric Theatre in Belfast. I thought 'Why the hell not?' and approached him. 'May I buy you a drink, Dr Fay?' He eyed me up and down and sighed theatrically: 'Beneath those whiskers do I discern the idle Longley?'

During the summer holidays Fay attended advanced study courses in Oxford and Cambridge. He came back from one given by the legendary Greek scholar Eduard Fraenkel to tell this teenager about the influence of primitive wedding ceremonies on the choruses of Aeschylus. He pushed me to the limits of my abilities. The Classics for him were character forming like long-distance running. Like playing chess, they were also about being clever. Thanks to the drilling I received at Inst, I was able to survive my first two undergraduate years at Trinity College Dublin without doing much work. My career as a lapsed classicist had begun. My Greek professor, the great W. B. Stanford, believed that the *Odyssey* and the *Iliad* had been sung or chanted, and bravely gave us a demonstration:

ἄνδρα μοι ἔννεπε, μοῦσα, πολύτροπον, ὃς μάλα πολλὰ
πλάγχθη, ἐπεὶ Τροίης ἱερὸν πτολίεθρον ἔπερσεν
πολλῶν δ᾽ ἀνθρώπων ἴδεν ἄστεα καὶ νόον ἔγνω,
πολλὰ δ᾽ ὅ γ᾽ ἐν πόντῳ πάθεν ἄλγεα ὃν κατὰ θυμόν,
ἀρνύμενος ἥν τε ψυχὴν καὶ νόστον ἑταίρων.

Stanford deepened my love of Homer as much through the speculations in his study *The Ulysses Theme* as through the scholarly notes at the back of his edition. I became obsessed with James Joyce's *Ulysses*. It was intoxicating to wander from a Stanford lecture on, say, the 'Circe' episode, to the dilapidated Turkish bathhouse on the street behind Trinity College and other nearby sites that Joyce had used as settings for his great novel. My earliest Homer-influenced poems were filtered through the shabby Dublin fanlights of *Ulysses*. Odysseus takes on the characteristics of a seedy Leopold Bloom:

When I sight you playing ball on the sand,
A suggestion of hair under your arms,
Or, in shallows, wearing only the waves,
I unpack strictly avuncular charms –
To lose these sea legs I walk on land ...

['Odyssey']

And Nausicaa is overshadowed by Gerty MacDowell:

You scarcely raise a finger to the tide.
Pavilions, those days-off at the seaside

Collapse about your infinite arrest –
He sees your cove more clearly than the rest.

['Nausicaa']

After these Joyce-inflected poems from the sixties, I didn't really get back onto the Homeric wavelength until 1989/90 – a gap of more than twenty years – when I wrote a cluster of poems based on Odysseus's complicated re-unions with his mother, father, nurse and dog. The first of these, 'Eurycleia', came disguised in prose as my *own* nurse, Lena Hardy. A country girl from County Fermanagh, Lena came to Belfast in 1939 to help my mother look after her twin babies while my father was off at the War. Lena became a surrogate mother. When she left at the end of the War, I was disconsolate. I celebrated her in a short memoir called *Tuppenny Stung*. Here is the first sentence: 'I began by loving the wrong woman.' It took me some time to realise that Lena was *my* Eurycleia. When I came to write the poem, the opening line of my memoir did not require much adjustment: 'I began like Odysseus by loving the wrong woman.' The old nurse bathes Odysseus and recognises him when she touches a telltale scar. Loving-kindness irradiates the story:

Such pain and happiness, her eyes filling with tears,
Her old voice cracking as she stroked his beard and whispered
'You are my baby boy for sure and I didn't know you
Until I had fondled my master's body all over.'

This poem matters to me because it sparked off the Homeric adventure of my fifties and sixties, my return to the Classics after a quarter of a century. From the outset, in my Homeric poems I pushed against the narrative momentum. The *Iliad* and the *Odyssey* are page-turners. We go on reading to find out what happens next. But in my poems I 'freeze-frame' passages to release their lyric potential.

A week after I had written 'Eurycleia' I was holidaying in a hilltop village in Tuscany. Leaning out of the bathroom window to admire the surrounding mountains I spotted an elderly neighbour tending his vines beyond the last houses. Old Cesare reminded me of my father, then of Odysseus's father. I had brought with me to Cardoso the two Loeb volumes of the *Odyssey* and E. V. Rieu's underrated translation. With these to assist my creakingly unpractised Greek, I wrote 'Laertes' quickly and with a sense of release. Laertes is in mourning for his son Odysseus. He doesn't realise that Odysseus is standing in front of him, alive and well. The poem begins:

> When he found Laertes alone on the tidy terrace, hoeing
> Around a vine, disreputable in his gardening duds,
> Patched and grubby, leather gaiters protecting his shins
> Against brambles, gloves as well, and, to cap it all,
> Sure sign of his deep depression, a goatskin duncher ...

The longer lines, sparked off by the Homeric hexameter, let loose new rhythms in my head. And 'duncher', the quaint Belfast dialect word for a flat cap (which caused some alarm among the fact-checkers of the *New Yorker* when the poem was published there) – fixed for me the tone of this fairly free version. The poem ends:

> ... Laertes recognised his son and, weak at the knees,
> Dizzy, flung his arms around the neck of great Odysseus
> Who drew the old man fainting to his breast and held him there
> And cradled like driftwood the bones of his dwindling father.

The eighteen lines make up one long swaying sentence. For reasons I don't fully understand the syntax of many of my poems unwinds through a single sentence. (Perhaps it has something to do with all that time spent on periodic structure in Latin and Greek prose composition.) I also seem obsessively reliant on symmetry. Three weeks after 'Laertes' I wrote a companion piece about Odysseus meeting his mother in the underworld. Another eighteen-line poem in one continuous sentence, 'Anticleia' begins with two long conditional subordinate clauses and ends as a question:

And if, having given her blood to drink and talked about home,
You lunge forward three times to hug her and three times
Like a shadow or idea she vanishes through your arms
And you ask her why she keeps avoiding your touch and weep
Because here is your mother and even here in Hades
You could comfort each other in a shuddering embrace,
Will she explain that the sinews no longer bind her flesh
And bones, that the irresistible fire has demolished these,
That the soul takes flight like a dream and flutters in the sky,
That this is what happens to human beings when they die?

I left out a fair amount of background material. I was not concerned with the narrative. I was looking for an intense lyric to set beside 'Laertes'. The two poems turned out to be the same length and that felt like some kind of endorsement, like a silversmith's hallmark. I compressed the stories to release the personal meaning. Homer enabled me to write belated lamentations for my mother and father.

Homer also empowered me to comment obliquely on the Northern Irish Troubles. I wrote 'Anticleia' when I was in a remote townland in County Mayo called Carrigskeewaun. The landscape there often looks like a sodden Ithaca. Odysseus would have recognised the white-washed farms and outbuildings. He would have understood the sticky intimate violence of our tawdry little civil war that was to drag on for thirty years. In Carrigskeewaun, with a cardboard box full of translations and commentaries, I started work on the episode where Odysseus slaughters the suitors. I had recently read *The Shankill Butchers*, a study by Martin Dillon of a psychopathic loyalist gang who tortured and murdered many Catholics. These horrors haunted the composition of 'The Butchers'. I admit to this with some reluctance because I do not want to be seen as the literal-minded besmircher of a great literary masterpiece. Lyric treatment of Book XXII's bloodthirsty ferocity demanded tumultuous syntax, twenty-eight fleet-footed alexandrine-like lines straining to the limit in one long sentence. I focused on the

similes – 'like fish', 'like a lion', 'like long-winged thrushes', 'like bats' –
and I Hibernicised my version with such details as the 'bog-meadow full
of bog-asphodels' and 'sheughs' (the Bog Meadows are in West Belfast
and 'sheugh' comes from the Irish for 'ditch'). My biggest liberty was to
skip Book XXIII and reconnect the frenzy of the bloodbath with the
eerie opening of Book XXIV. Here Hermes accompanies the suitors'
ghosts down into the underworld (in my version I include the souls of
the housemaids whom Homer seems to have forgotten about – my little
feminist gesture). I felt very close to Homer. Writing 'The Butchers' was an
electrifying experience. I worked on it through the night. I was shaking
when I read it aloud to my wife in the small hours:

> And when they had dragged Melanthios's corpse into the haggard
> And cut off his nose and ears and cock and balls, a dog's dinner,
> Odysseus, seeing the need for whitewash and disinfectant,
> Fumigated the house and the outhouses, so that Hermes
> Like a clergyman might wave the supernatural baton
> With which he resurrects or hypnotises those he chooses,
> And waken and round up the suitors' souls, and the housemaids',
> Like bats gibbering in the nooks of their mysterious cave
> When out of the clusters that dangle from the rocky ceiling
> One of them drops and squeaks, so their souls were bat-squeaks
> As they flittered after Hermes, their deliverer, who led them
> Along the clammy sheughs, then past the oceanic streams
> And the white rock, the sun's gatepost in that dreamy region,
> Until they came to a bog-meadow full of bog-asphodels
> Where the residents are ghosts or images of the dead.

Sometimes word-play on its own can inspire a translation – the
hidden depths of a pun. In 'The Butchers' there was no room for Phemios,
Ithaca's Poet-in-Residence, and Medon the toastmaster, a rather ridic-
ulous pair who have escaped the rage of Odysseus by hiding. I wanted
to give them a comic poem of their own in Ulster-Scots. The word for
'to clean', 'to set in order', is 'redd' in Ulster-Scots (it is still widely used in

Ulster). I visualised white walls splashed with blood. The act of cleansing is a bloody one. 'Redd' sparked off the poem 'Phemios & Medon'. Pleading for mercy the cringing poet:

> Makes a ram-stam for Odysseus, grammels his knees,
> Then bannies and bams wi this highfalutin blether.

I truffled through various Scots-English dictionaries (including the then recently published *Concise Ulster Dictionary* – a rumbustious treasure-trove full of words I was discouraged from using in Primary School) and I unearthed some marvellous words: 'scoot-hole', 'gabble-blooter', 'belly-bachelor'. I turned 'winged words' into 'highfalutin blether'. For the *wily* Odysseus 'long-headed' sounded just right. Homer's language is, after all, an amalgam of dialects. At the end of the poem Odysseus addresses the toastmaster Medon:

> Long-headed Odysseus smiles at him and says: 'Wheesht!
> You may thank Telemachos for this chance to wise up
> And pass on the message of oul decency. Go out
> And sit in the haggard away from this massacre,
> You and the well-spoken poet, while I redd the house.'
> They hook it and hunker fornenst the altar of Zeus,
> Afeard and skelly-eyed, keeking everywhere for death.

The violence towards the end of the *Odyssey* brings us back full circle to the warfare of the *Iliad*. The *Iliad* is probably our greatest poem about war and death. Poetry had to change after the *Iliad*. It did change, but it didn't get any better. A bit like music after J. S. Bach. Great works of art are packed with smaller works of art for opportunistic painters and poets and composers to purloin. I produced five reflections of the *Iliad* in 1994, mirror fragments. Some of these have a Northern Irish intonation – 'The Helmet' for instance, a short lyric about Hector's farewell to his wife and child. (The loyalist paramilitary leader Johnnie 'Mad Dog' Adair of the UDA referred to his son as 'Mad Pup'. He did, alas, come to

mind while I was writing this poem.) When Hector's helmet frightens
his baby son:

> His daddy laughed, his mammy laughed, and his daddy
> Took off the helmet and laid it on the ground to gleam,
> Then kissed the babbie and dandled him in his arms and
> Prayed that his son might grow up bloodier than him.

The magical simile with which Homer compares the campfires on
the plain of Troy to the night sky has often reminded me of County
Mayo where in the electric-light-free darkness I can gaze up into the
depths of the Milky Way. When I translated this passage it seemed
natural to include some place names and features from my corner of
the Mayo landscape:

> There are balmy nights – not a breath, constellations
> Resplendent in the sky around a dazzling moon –
> When a clearance high in the atmosphere unveils
> The boundlessness of space, and all the stars are out
> Lighting up hill-tops, glens, headlands, vantage
> Points like Tonakeera and Allaran where the tide
> Turns into Killary, where salmon run from the sea,
> Where the shepherd smiles on his luminous townland.
>
> ['The Campfires']

Occasionally a poem breaks free into the world at large. In August
1994 there were strong rumours that the IRA were about to declare a
ceasefire. I had been reading in Book XXIV the account of King Priam's
visit to Achilles's tent to beg for the body of his son Hector. Power shifts
from the mighty general to the old king who reminds Achilles of his own
father and awakens in him suppressed emotions of tenderness. Psychologically it feels pretty modern. I wanted to compress this scene's two-
hundred lines into a short lyric, publish it and make my minuscule
contribution to the peace process. I got started by tinkering with the

sequence of events. Priam kisses Achilles's hand at the *beginning* of their encounter. I put this at the *end* of my poem and inadvertedly created a rhyming couplet. Three quatrains followed. I sent my sonnet to the then literary editor of the *Irish Times*, John Banville, who called 'Stop Press' and published it on the Saturday immediately following the IRA's declaration of a ceasefire from midnight on 31 August 1994.

I

Put in mind of his own father and moved to tears
Achilles took him by the hand and pushed the old king
Gently away, but Priam curled up at his feet and
Wept with him until their sadness filled the building.

II

Taking Hector's corpse into his own hands Achilles
Made sure it was washed and, for the old king's sake,
Laid out in uniform, ready for Priam to carry
Wrapped like a present home to Troy at daybreak.

III

When they had eaten together, it pleased them both
To stare at each other's beauty as lovers might,
Achilles built like a god, Priam good-looking still
And full of conversation, who earlier had sighed:

IV

'I get down on my knees and do what must be done
And kiss Achilles' hand, the killer of my son.'

['Ceasefire']

The sort of lyric I write almost always makes its occasion in private. 'Ceasefire' was an exception. But it seems important to keep at a distance whatever political parallels the story may suggest. It was Homer who spoke to us across the millennia. I was only his mouthpiece.

III

Latin poetry is another 'wide expanse'. We find all the genres there –
epic, love lyric, elegy, satire. So far I have not followed my Homeric
experiments with translations from Virgil's *Aeneid*; rather, I have opted
for chamber music intimacies. As an undergraduate I was drawn to the
neurotic and strangely à la mode poetry of Sextus Propertius. I tried to
capture in English the ebb and flow of the Latin love elegy. In 'A Nightmare' I used a decasyllabic line (with risky enjambments) and a
straightforward rhyme scheme, ABAB. Propertius dreams that his lover
is drowning:

> Had they seen you then, the mermaids for envy
> Would have scolded you, so beautiful and
> One of them, a white girl from the blue sea,
> Loved by mermen and by men on the land.

In 'Cupid' the line lengths vary and the rhyme scheme is more demanding.
If he is destroyed by Cupid, the poet says, and with him:

> The little genius which is all I have to show,
> Who will celebrate the face and curls,
> The fingers and dark eyes of my girl,
> And who will sing of how softly her footsteps go?

In 1976 I met Betty Williams and Mairead Corrigan in a Belfast pub
shortly after they had won the Nobel Peace Prize. I congratulated them
on their great honour and on their movement's newspaper *Peace News*,
but suggested they were publishing feeble poems in it. 'If you don't like the
friggin poems, why don't you write one for us!' Betty Williams demanded.
That evening I opened my Loeb edition of Tibullus at – unbelievably –
'Quis fuit, horrendos primus qui protulit enses?' The coincidence gal-
vanised me and over a few intense days I wrote 'Peace'. I translated
Tibullus's opening lines as: 'Who was responsible for the very first arms

[35]

deal – / The man of iron who thought of marketing the sword?' I chose a ten-line stanza and risked being left with too few lines at the end, or too many. My gamble paid off. There are seven ten-line stanzas:

I want to live until the white hairs shine above
A pensioner's memories of better days. Meanwhile
I would like peace to be my partner on the farm,
Peace personified: oxen under the curved yoke;
Compost for the vines, grape-juice turning into wine,
Vintage years handed down from father to son;
Hoe and ploughshares gleaming, while in some dark corner
Rust keeps the soldier's grisly weapons in their place;
The labourer steering his wife and children home
In a hay cart from the fields, a trifle sozzled.

In 'Peace' each stanza is a self-contained argument. I end the poem with a flourish that stretches but does not, I trust, distort the Latin:

As for me, I want a woman
To come and fondle my ears of wheat and let apples
Overflow between her breasts. I shall call her Peace.

In 1992 I was invited by Michael Hofmann and James Lasdun to contribute to a collection of versions from Ovid's *Metamorphoses*. For *After Ovid* I translated one of the loveliest stories in the world, the tale of faithful Baucis and Philemon's encounter with the gods and how Jupiter rewards their hospitality and generosity of spirit. I began at the end of the poem and worked backwards. Again, as with 'Peace', I was in luck. The story in my version progresses through eighteen self-contained five-line stanzas, many of them little chronicles of workaday metamorphosis: the embers that turn 'leaves and dry bark' into flames; the cabbage and smoked bacon 'simmered in bubbling water to make a stew'; the sofa and mattress that a simple coverlet transforms into a throne for the gods. The old couple's humility and loving-kindness light up the story and throw a halo around mundane objects. These 'every-day miracles' set the scene for the poem's supernatural wonders: the wine jug that 'filled itself up again'; the cottage that 'became a church'; and finally, the old couple's transfiguration as their wish to die together is granted: 'As tree-tops overgrew their smiles they called in unison / "Goodbye, my dear"'. I did not leave out one of Ovid's affectionate details. And at the close I added a couple of my own:

Two trees are grafted together where their two bodies stood.
I add my flowers to bouquets in the branches by saying
'Treat those whom God loves as your local gods – a blackthorn
Or a standing stone. Take care of caretakers and watch
Over the nightwatchman and the nightwatchman's wife.'

['Baucis and Philemon']

It is surprising to find in *Metamorphoses* this unironical celebration of a long happy marriage. In their introduction Hofmann and Lasdun give us an astonishing list of what we can normally expect from Ovid's great work: 'holocaust, plague, sexual harassment, rape, incest, seduction, pollution, sex-change, suicide, hetero- and homosexual love, torture, war, child-battering, depression and intoxication.' I agree with them when they say that the stories 'offer a mythical key to most of the more extreme forms of human behaviour and suffering.' I now wanted to explore the weirder zones.

In 'According to Pythagoras' I further compressed the selection Ovid made from the philosopher's teachings. What by modern experimental standards would be judged bad science works wonderfully well as surreal poetry:

There's a theory that in the grave the backbone rots
Away and the spinal cord turns into a snake.

Occasionally, as in the reference to the hyena's genitalia, an uncanny scientific accuracy takes us by surprise: 'the female mounted by a male / Just minutes before, becomes a male herself.' (In real life the female hyena does indeed flaunt false male genitals: a power game.) Both the scientific and the surreal appealed to Ovid, and to me. When I had finished 'According to Pythagoras' I counted, to my dismay, twenty-nine lines. With an extra line the poem would have divided perfectly into three ten-line stanzas: my hunger for symmetry again. My wife reminded me of a leitmotif from Douglas Adams's glorious post-Ovidian fantasy *Dirk Gently's Holistic Detective Agency*, and for reasons numerical and poetical I appropriated it:

> The fundamental interconnectedness of all things
> Is incredible enough, but did you know that
> Hyenas change sex ...


IV

Latin and Greek have been fundamental to my imaginative development. Versions that reflect my preoccupations at a deep level feel to me like my own poems, especially when I combine free rendition of source texts with original lines. An example of this is 'The Evening Star', written in memory of Catherine Mercer (1994–6):

> The day we buried your two years and two months
> So many crocuses and snowdrops came out for you
> I tried to isolate from those galaxies one flower:
> A snowdrop appeared in the sky at dayligone,
> The evening star, the star in Sappho's epigram
> Which brings back everything that shiny daybreak
> Scatters, which brings the sheep and brings the goat
> And brings the wean back home to her mammy.

Without Sappho's exquisite fragment, lightly Hibernicised, and the loveliest word I know for evening, 'dayligone', an Ulster dialect word, I could not have broached this heartrending subject.

A group of Greek poets and a group of Latin poets provide me with a coda. *Snow Water* includes a poem called 'The Group', a suite of seven short pieces derived from the Loeb *Greek Lyric* series. Each stars a minor poet – Lamprocles, Myrtis, Telesilla, Charixenna. The more obscure the poet, the more I was attracted. Next to nothing is known about most of them. Teetering on the verge of almost total oblivion, they hang on in a few fragments, or as one-liner gags in Aristophanes, or as footnotes in some ancient critic's essay. I chose the title, 'The Group', mischievously, as a red herring which is meant to put researchers of the Belfast Group off the trail for as long as possible. Some readers will look for Seamus Heaney behind 'Ion of Chios, the prize-winning poet' or Medbh McGuckian, perhaps, behind 'hypochondriacal Telesilla'. But they will be missing the point. In its light-hearted way, 'The Group' is concerned with the poetic trade in general and what it involves: careerism, fashion, fame, obscurity, integrity, contamination, factionalism, camaraderie, intrigue, idealism, transitoriness, failure. Groups of poets do not change all that much over the centuries. Charixenna, the last poet in 'The Group', represents us all:

Oblivious to being out of date,
Which of us will not appear as dopey
As Charixenna, oldfashioned pipe-player
And composer of oldfashioned tunes
And, according to some, a poet too?

In contrast, most of the poets in my Latin group are very well-known. In his *Tristia* the miserably exiled Ovid gives us a tantalising glimpse of his poetic friends far away in Rome. He misses them, and writes warmly about Propertius and Horace and regrets that Tibullus's early death thwarted their friendship. Virgil he only saw, he says 'Vergilium vidi tantum' ('but, yes, they all knew each other'). In addition to these immortals Ovid names three other members of the coterie who have completely faded away: Macer, Ponticus and Bassus. Three busy literary careers, and hardly a syllable survives. I used Ovid's lines as the basis for a poem I have called 'Remembering the Poets' – it is a playful sonnet about the friendship of poets. Unavoidably, the personalities of my *own* brilliant contemporaries kept crowding in from the back of my mind. The poem expresses brotherly love for *them* and for the poets I converse with across the millennia:

> As a teenage poet I idolised the poets, doddery
> Macer trying out his *Ornithogonia* on me,
> And the other one about herbal cures for snake bites,
> Propertius, my soul mate, love's polysyllabic
> Pyrotechnical laureate reciting reams by heart,
> Ponticus straining to write The Long Poem, Bassus
> (Sorry for dropping names) iambic to a fault,
> Horace hypnotising me with songs on the guitar,
> Virgil, our homespun internationalist, sighted
> At some government reception, and then Albius
> Tibullus strolling in the woods a little while
> With me before he died, his two slim volumes
> An echo from the past, a melodious complaint
> That reaches me here, the last of the singing line.

*A transcript of a lecture given in Trinity College Dublin on 28 January 2009.*

# The West

When we were thirteen or fourteen my parents took my twin brother
and me on a caravan holiday to Donegal. Donegal, which is *in* the North
but *of* the West, might be considered an ideal location for the beginnings
of my spiritual education. We were headed in our caravan for Downings
on the Rosguill Peninsula. My father misread the map and we parked in
the dark by the roadside just beyond Carrigart and only a few miles from
our destination. I woke in the morning to a revelation, my first glimpse
of wilderness in the Atlantic light. At that moment I discovered my soul-
landscape. Close to the seashore at Downings we camped on some
grassy machair, our caravan an eyesore for miles around. I would sit on
the headland and write ecstatic letters to friends in Belfast about the
view across Sheephaven Bay to Marble Strand and Muckish (the first of
my holy mountains). Looking back at my passionate desire to share the
landscape, I think I can recognise the incipient poet – someone for
whom no experience is complete until he or she has written about it,
someone who would hope to share the experience with others.

The first great yellow strand to fill my imagination was Tra-na-Rossan.
The Atlantic Drive winds uphill beyond the village of Downings. It turns
rocky corners until, stretching out below and beyond, there is Tra-na-
Rossan. The strand inspired a nineteen-year-old's first love poem to the
Western (or the Northwestern) landscape:

> We walked on Tra-na-rossan strand;
> the Atlantic winds were wiping the heat
> from the August sun and the stretching sand
> was cold beneath our naked feet ...

> ['After Tra-na-Rossan']

In 1965, my wife and I hitchhiked with Derek Mahon around Connemara. Life in Belfast had been demanding and painful because a friend was having a breakdown. Were we drawn perhaps to the *idea* of the place? 'Connemara' – and here I quote Tim Robinson – 'Connemara – the name drifts across the mind like cloud shadows on a mountainside, or expands and fades like circles on a lake after a trout has risen.' For Louis MacNeice as a child the West glimmered in family conversation and at the back of his mind: 'The very name Connemara seemed too rich for any ordinary place. It appeared to be a country of windswept open spaces and mountains blazing with whins and seas that were never quiet. But I was not to visit Achill or Connemara until I had left school. So for many years I lived on a nostalgia for somewhere I had never been.'

I still feel a bit like that, even though our 1965 trip turned out to be a prelude to hundreds of journeys along the roads to Westport and Louisburgh and Leenane. In Galway we boarded the steamer for Inishmore – a very rough crossing – there were no stabilisers on the boat – belowdecks Mahon and I fought off seasickness with medicinal brandies. In Kilronan we hired a jaunting car that took us to our guest house. When we told him we didn't speak Irish, our driver sighed: 'Oh you're lost. You're Lost.' Was he joking? Perhaps we *were* lost. It rained most of the time and we huddled in an attic bedroom in our inflammable sleeping bags, chain-smoking. Between showers we walked around the rocky fields in flashing, soul-irradiating light. Our brief sojourn would become part of my inner mythology, and part of Mahon's. We felt sad leaving the island. My eventual response was 'Leaving Inishmore', the first West-inspired poem of mine to survive: here are the middle two stanzas:

> Miles from the brimming enclave of the bay
> I hear again the Atlantic's voices,
> The gulls above as we pulled away –
> So munificent their final noises
> These are the broadcasts from our holiday.

Oh, the crooked walkers on that tilting floor!
And the girls singing on the upper deck
Whose hair took the light like a downpour –
Interim nor change of scene shall shipwreck
Those folk on the move between shore and shore.

Derek Mahon and I returned to the Aran Islands the following Easter
– Easter 1966. On a whim we left the steamer when it anchored in the
bay and were rowed in a currach to the smallest of the islands, Inisheer.
We spotted on the shore someone of bohemian appearance, pacing up
and down, clearly anxious about his mail. We introduced ourselves. He
had read our early poems in the *Dublin Magazine* where *we* had read
his short story 'Epithalamion'. The friendly stranger, Tom MacIntyre,
was living on the island with his young family. He persuaded us to stay
and arranged our lodgings with a witty woman who served us with
boiled bacon three times a day. On Good Friday, Derek and I were very
moved when we witnessed the islanders, in their best tweeds, walking
on their knees over the stone flags into the church. Five years later in
'Letter to Derek Mahon' my perspective on all this may reflect the
beginning of the Troubles. I describe us as:

… tongue-tied
Companions of the island's dead
In the graveyard among the dunes,
Eavesdroppers on conversations
With a Jesus who spoke Irish –
We were strangers in that parish …

It is striking that my first collection and the first collections of Derek
Mahon and Seamus Heaney all contain poems about the Aran Islands.
As visitors, as strangers, as outsiders, the three of us in our different
ways were following in the footsteps of J. M. Synge. Perhaps at this
point I should own up to borrowing a sentence from *The Aran Islands*
for a poem of my own about Inisheer. Here is Synge's sentence: 'There

is only one bit and saddle in the island, which are used by the priest, who rides from the chapel to the pier when he has held the service on Sunday.' And here is the rather satirical opening stanza of my poem 'The Island':

The one saddle and bit on the island
We set aside for every second Sunday
When the priest rides slowly up from the pier.
Afterwards his boat creaks into the mist.
Or he arrives here nine times out of ten
With the doctor. They will soon be friends.

In 'Synge on Aran' Seamus Heaney invokes Synge as a poetic role-model:

There
he comes now, a hard pen
scraping in his head;
the nib filed on a salt wind
and dipped in the keening sea.

And in 'Lovers on Aran' Heaney beautifully symbolises sexual reciprocity in terms of the landscape:

Did sea define the land or land the sea?
Each drew new meaning from the waves' collision.
Sea broke on land to full identity.

In 'Epitaph for Robert Flaherty', Derek Mahon makes the great American filmmaker say of Aran:

The relief to be out of the sun,
To have come north once more
To my islands of dark ore
Where winter is so long

Only a little light
Gets through, and that perfect.

And in 'Recalling Aran' Mahon seems to view the place itself as an
artefact, as some kind of aesthetic absolute (both his Aran poems use
the word 'perfect'):

A dream of limestone in sea-light
Where gulls have placed their perfect prints.
Reflection in that final sky
Shames vision into simple sight –
Into pure sense, experience.
Four thousand miles away tonight,
Conceived beyond such innocence,
I clutch the memory still, and I
Have measured everything with it since.

The Aran poems of our youth do not seem to me to be escapist. We were
drawn to what in my salute to 'Dr Johnson on the Hebrides' I call 'the
far-flung outposts of experience.' We yearned for revelation that could
well prove unbalancing in its intensity, or, to quote another early poem,
'The Hebrides' – for me the Irish and Scottish west sometimes converge
– we coveted 'the privilege / Of vertigo.'

It is extraordinary how the West continues to draw poets in a spiritual, non-material way. What Yeats began with 'The Wanderings of
Oisin' is far from exhausted. Gerald Dawe's most recent collection, for
instance, is called *Points West*. For Louis MacNeice in his rhapsodic
'Western Landscape':

... this land
Is always more than matter – as a ballet
Dancer is more than body. The West of Ireland
Is brute and ghost at once.

Richard Murphy first attracted the attention of us 'Western wannabes' with his majestic narratives 'Sailing to an Island' and 'The Cleggan Disaster'. Over the years I have been inspired by his consummate nature poems – 'Storm Petrel', 'Corncrake', 'Sea Holly', 'Seals at High Island'. Paul Durcan often looks West when he contemplates visionary alternatives to a dystopian Ireland. In 'The Seal of Burrishoole', for example, he counters dark forces by imagining an ideal Western burial as a form of spiritual purgation:

Bury me in the estuary
When the tide has gone out
Uncovering the track;
Under wine-red boughs of mid-winter
And faithful yellow furze;
Where seaweed is all over
And six cows stand apart from one another
Along the spine of the drumlin,
And a sea breeze blows from the west
And in the gap of the estuary
The seal of my death
Poised on rock as it always has been.

My own youthful passion grew into a lifetime's obsession. When I counted them up recently, I was surprised to find that one third of my poems are set in South-West Mayo. This is thanks to David Cabot, the great Irish ornithologist, who allows me to stay in his remote cottage and open my mind to the endless intricacies of the landscape and the Atlantic weather. I fell in love with Carrigskeewaun the first time I saw it – nearly forty years ago – from the turn in the road above Thallabawn – a great sandy arena with a meandering channel, dunes and the lakes and the cottage. I have been going there with my family since 1970. My wife and I have carried each of our three children through the Owennadornaun River and the tidal channel, then across the stretch of sandy grazing behind the dunes to the rickety gate, over the low bridge where brown trout and elvers wait, and up the last rising curves of the path to the white cottage in its little bumpy square of fuchsia hedges and stone walls – and all of this against the backdrop of Mweelrea (my second holy mountain). The first fruits of this love affair were six short topographical lyrics – 'The Mountain', 'The Strand', 'The Lake' and so on – a sequence dedicated to David and Penny Cabot and called, of course, 'Carrigskeewaun'. The sequence closes with 'The Lake', which hopes to make room for all of us outsiders:

Though it will duplicate at any time
The sheep and cattle that wander there,
For a few minutes every evening
Its surface seems tilted to receive
The sun perfectly, the mare and her foal,
The heron, all such special visitors.

In his essay on 'Contemporary Irish poetry' in the *Field Day Anthology* Declan Kiberd castigates 'the number of poems set on the Aran Islands, or in West Kerry, or on the coast of Donegal – all written by artists who act like self-conscious tourists in their own country.' This kind of thinking makes me feel excluded. So I find reassuring what Derek Mahon says in his essay 'MacNeice in England and Ireland': 'There is a belief, prevalent since the time of Thomas Davis, that Irish poetry, to be Irish, must somehow express the National Aspirations; and MacNeice's failure to do so ... is one of the reasons for his final exclusion from the charmed circle, known and feared the world over, of Irish Poets. "A tourist in his own country", it has been said, with the implication that this is somehow discreditable. But of what sensitive person is the same not true?' I also find it reassuring that Máirtín Ó Direáin wrote a 'Homage to John Millington Synge'. At the end of the poem he stresses that 'the words' of his people 'will live on in an alien tongue.'

Even Seamus Heaney, for me, hits a wrong note when he criticises the great naturalist Lloyd Praeger: 'Praeger's point of view is visual, geological, not like Kavanagh's, emotional and definitive. His eye is regulated by laws of aesthetics, by the disciplines of physical geography, and not, to borrow a phrase from Wordsworth, by the primary laws of our nature, the laws of feeling.' Kiberd and Heaney seem to circumscribe who can speak of the West and how it can be spoken of. Praeger's biographer, Seán Lysaght, is surely right when he puts Praeger alongside Yeats, Synge, Lady Gregory and Douglas Hyde as one of the culture-givers of the revival – the nationalist revival. Just as others had turned to archaeology and folklore to rediscover the roots of culture, Praeger, says Lysaght, helped in 'the establishment of Ireland as a biological and geographical territory with an identity of its own.'

Sometimes I find it impossible *not* to view the Western landscape through the eyes of two aesthetic outsiders from Belfast, two painters: Paul Henry and Gerard Dillon. Almost single-handedly Henry created a vision of the West, especially Achill Island, which, with its turfstacks and thatched roofs and currachs, persists in a sort of semi-official way as the state's self-image (or one version of it). At a profounder level, sea and sky do actually combine on certain days in the West as though in a Paul Henry composition. Gerard Dillon who died in 1971 hailed from the Lower Falls district of Belfast, which he depicted magically; but it was in Connemara that he found his soul – on Inishlacken and in the area around Roundstone. My elegy for him begins:

You walked, all of a sudden, through
The rickety gate which opens
To a scatter of curlews,
An acre of watery light...

['In Memory of Gerard Dillon']

In an *Irish Times* review of his last Belfast exhibition I called him 'the poet of Irish painting' – an overwrought phrase perhaps, but he embodies for me the very idea of the poet as close observer of the natural world. In the poem I describe him as

... an eye
Taking in the beautiful predators –
Cats on the windowsill, birds of prey

And, between the diminutive fields,
A dragonfly, wings full of light
Where the road narrows to the last farm.

Gerard Dillon showed me how to find my way from Belfast to the beautiful places. There have been other guides – Synge of course, pioneering ecologists like Praeger and the field naturalists, the Edwardian giants (many of them from the North) who carried out the Clare Island Survey of 1909 to 1911. This was the world's first major inventory of a single geographical location. These naturalists were also among the first to recognise the scientific importance of the Burren – that extraordinary place where arctic and Mediterranean plants co-mingle. Amusingly – and here I quote from Cilian Roden's essay in *The Book of the Burren* – two unionist naturalists joked that the blue gentian, white mountain avens and red bloody cranesbill on a Burren hillside were a marvellous reflection of the Union flag 'on the western extremity of the United Kingdom.'

I revere the great geographers of more recent times – Frank Mitchell from Trinity College, Estyn Evans from Queen's University, whom I was lucky enough to meet. I would add to my list brilliant contemporaries such as Charles Nelson with whom I have botanised in County Clare, and Tim Robinson, the Western seaboard's greatest cartographer and philosopher, with whom I have walked around Inishlacken in search of Gerard Dillon's ghost and freshwater wells among the seaweed. Certain books are my bibles: *The Way That I Went, The Aran Islands, Irish Folk Ways, Reading the Irish Landscape, The Burren: A Companion to the Wildflowers of an Irish Limestone Wilderness, Setting Foot in Connemara, Sailing to an Island.*

David Cabot, the custodian of Carrigskeewaun, published in 1999, in the wonderful Collins New Naturalist Library series, his compendious study of Ireland's diverse habitats – from the mountains and peat lands to the sea and the islands. It is called *Ireland*. Four years later his neighbour and our close friend Michael Viney brought out with the Smithsonian Institute his own major study called – yes – *Ireland*. In it he examines the intricate balance of plants and animals, geology, and climate. It seems to me astonishing that in the neighbouring townlands of Carrigskeewaun and Thallabawn, on either side of the little Owennadornaun River, a minute apart as the raven flies, two great naturalists should create their masterworks. And that's not the end of it. In 2008 Michael Viney (who of course is also celebrated for his influential column 'Another Life' in the *Irish Times*) co-authored with Ethna Viney *Ireland's Ocean: A Natural History* which wonderfully extends the horizons of the Western seaboard into the sea. And he has just published *Wild Mayo*, a vivid guide for layman and visitor. David Cabot's second New Naturalist volume has also recently appeared – *Wildfowl* – a scholarly tome devoted to one of his lifelong obsessions. Cabot and Viney share their landscape with me. It has been my privilege and education to plod along behind them. To the cairn of books I would of course love to add my own *Collected Poems*.

The plants and the animals were what first involved me in Mayo. It was some time before I wrote about the people who live there. 'Mayo Monologues' are four psychologically dark portraits of fictional neighbours – composite characterisations that convey my view (at the time) of human beings in the landscape. In 'Self-heal', the third portrait, a virginal young schoolteacher is molested by a backward boy, to whom she has been teaching the names of flowers:

> I wasn't frightened and still I don't know why,
> But I ran from him in tears to tell them.
> I heard how every day for one whole week
> He was flogged with a blackthorn, then tethered
> In the hayfield. I might have been the cow
> Whose tail he would later dock with shears,
> And he the ram tangled in barbed wire
> That he stoned to death when they set him free.

I used to consider 'Mayo Monologues' excessively bleak, but not any more, not after so many recent revelations of depravity. Nevertheless, to this day, if I meet on the roads any of the people who might have contributed even a fragment to these composite portraits, I avoid their eyes. At readings I rarely recite 'Mayo Monologues'. I wasn't able to return to this communal zone until I'd got to know Joe O'Toole, one of the few local smallholders who ever admitted to me a love of the wild flowers and the birds – a love which brought us together:

> His way of seeing me safely across the duach
> Was to leave his porch light burning, its sparkle
> Shifting from widgeon to teal on Corragaun Lake.

I was downcast when he died:

> This morning on the burial mound at Templedoomore
> Encircled by a spring tide and taking in
> Cloonaghmanagh and Claggan and Carrigskeewaun,
> The townlands he'd wandered tending cows and sheep,
> I watched a dying otter gaze right through me
> At the islands in Clew Bay, as though it were only
> Between hovers and not too far from the holt.
>
> ['Between Hovers']

'Hover' is the exquisite English word for an otter's temporary resting place. The poem is called 'Between Hovers'. I suppose I see myself as hovering in the West too, and my poems as 'hovers'. Like many an elegy, 'Between Hovers' is also a kind of love poem. In my version of the West, love poem and elegy tend to get confused: the erotic and the sorrowful meld together. In 'Above Dooaghtry' (from *Snow Water*) Thanatos makes room for Eros as I give instructions for my funeral and describe the promontory fort where I want my ashes to be scattered:

> Let boulders at the top encircle me,
> Neither a drystone wall nor a cairn, space
> For the otter to die and the mountain hare

To lick snow stains from her underside,
A table for the peregrine and ravens,

A prickly double-bed as well, nettles
And carline-thistles, a sheeps' wool pillow,
So that, should she decide to join me there,
Our sandy dander to Allaran Point
Or Tonakeera will take forever.

I am still only scratching the surface of this small townland. Every time I leave, I wonder will there be any more Mayo poems; but the poems keep arriving. My forthcoming collection, *A Hundred Doors*, will contain another *eighteen*– more than ever – and I haven't finished the book yet. Not just for me but for other poets – Richard Murphy, Paul Durcan, Moya Cannon, Mary O'Malley – the West prompts more than just one kind of poem. As a genre the 'Western poem' can be infinitely capacious. I love Moya Cannon's cosmic Western poem 'Night' which ends with her staring up into the starry sky at:

... our windy, untidy loft
where old people had flung up old junk
they'd thought might come in handy,
ploughs, ladles, bears, lions, a clatter of heroes,
a few heroines, a path for the white cow, a swan
and, low down, almost within reach,
Venus, completely unfazed by the frost.

Carrigskeewaun provides me with the template for experiencing all other places and keeps me sensitive, I hope, to the nuances of locality. The human habitat in that part of Mayo is precarious, isolated, and vulnerable: its history complex. The landscape is haunted by grown-over potato-drills, the ghosts of lazy-beds abandoned during the Famine. The bones of the landscape make me feel in my own bones how provisional dwelling and home are. In 'Remembering Carrigskeewaun'

I say: 'Home is a hollow between the waves, / A clump of nettles, feathery winds ...'

In the Mayo poems I am not writing about a cosy community. Nor do I dwell among the calls of water birds and the psychedelic blaze of summer flowers to escape from Ulster's political violence. I want light from Carrigskeewaun to irradiate the Northern confusion. In Irish poetry 'the West' is not a pastoral domain outside history and violence. Think of Yeats's 'Meditations in Time of Civil War', or 'The Closing Album' by Louis MacNeice, poised on the brink of the Second World War. Paul Durcan often returns to the West in his critiques of contemporary Irish society. The Civil War, the Anglo-Irish War, two World Wars, the Troubles have all been refracted through the West. Although I called my very first Mayo poem 'The West', it is as much about the North. Here I am sitting in the cottage trying to listen through bad radio reception for news from Belfast:

> Beneath a gas-mantle that the moths bombard,
> Light that powders at a touch, dusty wings,
> I listen for news through the atmospherics,
> A crackle of sea-wrack, spinning driftwood,
> Waves like distant traffic, news from home ...

A later poem, 'The Ice-Cream Man', also brings together the two parts of Ireland I love the most – Belfast and the Western seaboard. On the Lisburn Road (where I live) the IRA murdered the man in the ice-cream shop. I had been away botanising in the Burren where I had written down in a notebook the names of all the wild flowers I could identify in one day. On my return home I learned of the murder; and my younger daughter Sarah told me that she had bought with her pocket money a bunch of carnations to lay outside the shop. I arranged the lovely flower-names from my notebook into a kind of aural wreath to place beside her bouquet. The poem is addressed to Sarah:

Rum and raisin, vanilla, butterscotch, walnut, peach:
You would rhyme off the flavours. That was before
They murdered the ice-cream man on the Lisburn Road
And you bought carnations to lay outside his shop.
I named for you all the wild flowers of the Burren
I had seen in one day: thyme, valerian, loosestrife,
Meadowsweet, tway blade, crowfoot, ling, angelica,
Herb Robert, marjoram, cow parsley, sundew, vetch,
Mountain avens, wood sage, ragged robin, stitchwort,
Yarrow, lady's bedstraw, bindweed, bog pimpernel.

I mean that catalogue to go on forever, like a prayer. The murder of the ice-cream man violates all nature. The poem is also, partly, an elegy for the flowers themselves, which are under increasing threat.

The whole island is under threat: contaminated lakes, fish-kills, ruthless overgrazing, 'bungalow blight', chemical overkill, building on flood plains, oil spills, inappropriately sited motorways. We are methodically turning beauty spots into eyesores. Even Carrigskeewaun is changing. The stony boreen that leads to the Owennadornaun River has been tarmacadamed. Where we used to wade with our bundles there is now a concrete bridge. We might have seen dippers and sandmartins and sandpipers there, and, in the meadow beyond, butterfly orchids. But the meadow has been turned into a carpark. When a neighbour asked me: 'And how do you like your lovely new carpark, Michael?', I couldn't believe she wasn't joking. Is Nature joking when gale-force winds blow over the two thoughtfully provided Portaloos?

I have a radiant memory of kneeling with my friend the botanical artist Raymond Piper to examine the rare dense-flowered orchid, *neotinea maculata*, in the Burren. We looked up from the peculiar little plant across a magically disappearing turlough to the contours of Mullaghmore (the third of my holy mountains). I don't come closer than this to religious experience. Against the advice of local and national and international environmental organisations, the Office of Public

Works was planning in 1999 to build an interpretative centre close to Mullaghmore. This was unnecessary because a centre already existed not too far away. It was also potentially catastrophic. Massive road-widening would have been required to facilitate the tankering-in of fresh water and the tankering-out of sewage. Into the most fragile and intricate of underground water systems the OPW was planning to sink a gigantic septic tank.

Raymond Piper and I got involved in what the *Irish Times* called 'The Battle of Mullaghmore'. We wrote letters to the papers. Raymond deplored 'unnecessary despoliation' and 'irreversible destruction'. I risked sounding boastful or pompous when I said: 'I am a poet whose work is currently represented on the Leaving Certificate syllabus. Many of my poems celebrate the landscape of the West of Ireland. Their very subject-matter is threatened by the absence of intelligent environmental policies.' I pleaded with the minister responsible at the time (Síle de Valera) to listen to the experts, and I asked: 'Does she really want her monument to be a public lavatory in the Garden of Eden?' In January, at the beginning of the millennium, Raymond and I drove down to Clare to take part in a demonstration. This was the first and last time either of us had spoken from the back of a lorry. Out of this commotion my 'Burren Prayer' was born:

Gentians and lady's bedstraw embroider her frock.
Her pockets are full of sloes and juniper berries.

Quaking-grass panicles monitor her heartbeat.
Her reflection blooms like mudwort in a puddle.

Sea lavender and Irish eyebright at Poll Salach,
On Black Head saxifrage and mountain-everlasting.

*Our Lady of the Fertile Rocks, protect the Burren.*
*Protect the Burren, Our Lady of the Fertile Rocks.*

The campaign was a success and work on the interpretative centre was abandoned. But our January protest had been met by angry counter-demonstrators. The construction of the centre would have generated short-term employment. Who were we and what business was it of ours? When we returned for some peaceable botanising, we were confronted with 'Keep Out' and 'Trespassers will be Prosecuted' signs. Our campaign had succeeded but at the cost of dividing the community and making visitors like ourselves unwelcome. Here again, we have the issue of who is entitled to speak about or for the West.

Damaged relations are gradually being repaired by the visionary work of Brendan Dunford and the Burrenbeo Trust. The Trust (of which I am a proud patron) aims to promote the self-sustaining conservation of the Burren. It recognises local farmers as the lifeblood of the region and the best guardians of its heritage. The famous wild flowers are, after all, a by-product of sensitively balanced farming activity over many years.

Raymond Piper died in July 2007. At his funeral I began my eulogy with lines from Christopher Smart's exuberant *Jubilate Agno* – lines which encapsulate everything I'm trying to say. Raymond Piper might be speaking them:

For flowers are good both for the living and the dead.
For there is a language of flowers.
For elegant phrases are nothing but flowers.
For flowers are peculiarly the poetry of Christ.

In my elegy for Raymond I recall some of our orchid odysseys. On one of these he took me to the Saltee Islands to look for insular hybrids. We hired a small fishing smack called *Mystical Rose*. Here are the last two stanzas of 'Cloud Orchid':

Undistracted in your greenhouse-
Studio by caterpillar
Droppings from the mimosa tree

That twisted overhead, you
Gazed up through the branches and
The broken pane imagining
Your last flower portrait – 'for flowers
Are good both for the living
And the dead' – the minuscule
Cloud Orchid that grows in the rain
Forest's misty canopy.

The rusty fuse you brought home
From a specific hummock
In Carrigskeewaun – autumn
Lady's-tresses – yet to flower
Under your greenhouse's moony
Glass in Belfast – do you want
Me to move it from the sill
Onto the ground for moisture
Or re-pot it or hire, as once
We did, *Mystical Rose*
And chug out to the Saltees?

A cultural version of Alzheimer's disease menaces what we now like to call 'our heritage'. It could well be the end of our species. We shall die if we let the wild flowers die. Some years ago I gave a reading at the local secondary school in Louisburgh. If it hadn't been for the poems and an RTÉ documentary Cabot and Viney had made about my Mayo sojourns, many of the children wouldn't have believed that herons and otters and stoats and falcons do indeed live just a few miles down the road in Carrigskeewaun and Thallabawn. Very few of the children had visited the area. On our own walks across the fields we hardly ever meet anyone – no local children at play – except an occasional shepherd perhaps. So last summer it was an intense pleasure to show my first grandson the wild flowers of Mayo. Our children now carry *their* children through the tidal channel to Carrigskeewaun. All five grandchildren have stayed in the cottage. And all five have inspired poems. 'The Fold' is for Catherine, the youngest:

> Why would the ewes and their lambs
> Assemble as though hypnotised
> Around the cottage? Do they sense
> A storm on its way? Or a fox?
> Darkness and quiet are folding
> All the sheep of Carrigskeewaun,
> Their fleeces lustrous, long wool
> For a baby's comfort-blanket,
> For Catherine asleep in her crib
> This midnight, our lambing-time.

In the cottage I often think of the first folk to live there, the O'Tooles who came from Inishdeigil, a tiny island at the mouth of the Killary. I can't imagine how they survived in such isolation. Mary O'Toole had eleven children on the island – without the aid of doctor or midwife. The state eventually provided the family with the cottage at Carrigskeewaun. In her new home Mary O'Toole would say: 'Now I can walk anywhere!' The thirteen O'Tooles were bilingual, played musical instruments, sang, and told stories. Their new home soon became famous as a ceilidh house. Folk came visiting from miles around. Some even rowed from Connemara in their currachs across the Killary for the music and a seat at the hearth. The Carrigskeewaun cottage is no longer a ceilidh house, alas. A poem by me will have to do instead. Here is the second half of 'Ceilidh':

> The thirteen O'Tooles are singing about everything.
> Their salty eggs are cherished for miles around.
> There's a hazel copse near the lake without a name.
> Dog violets, sorrel, wood spurge are growing there.
> On Inishdeigil there's a well of the purest water.
> Is that Arcturus or a faraway outhouse light?
> The crescent moon's a coracle for Venus. Look

Through the tide and over the Owennadornaun
Are shouldered the coffins of the thirteen O'Tooles.

We can be so parochial in our sense of time and space. In the words of Tim Robinson 'the geographies over which we are so suicidally passionate are ... fleeting expressions of the earth's face.' In the first poem in *A Hundred Doors*, I describe David Cabot alone in Carrigskeewaun for the millennium:

My friend sits at the hearth keeping the cottage warm ...
He has kept for this evening firewood that is very old.
Bog deal's five thousand years make the room too hot.

['Call']

We are also being parochial when we ignore the great migrations taking place – in more senses than one – 'above our heads' and the other heroic odysseys beneath the waves. In a poem called 'The Wren' I describe Carrigskeewaun as 'a townland whooper swans / From the tundra remember, and the Saharan / Wheatear.' Carrigskeewaun is not really a 'remote corner': it is a focal point, a nerve centre. When I walked with my friend the painter Jeffrey Morgan along Thallabawn Strand for the first time, we saw bottlenose dolphins in Clew Bay, then an otter capering out of the tide at Allaran Point. As we left for the cottage, five whooper swans circled above us on their way from Iceland to nearby Dooaghtry Lake.

During my years of visiting Carrigskeewaun, I have tried to 'sing about everything'. I have written poems there that touch on the Great War, the Holocaust, and the Troubles. The place has given me love poems, elegies, prayers, lullabies. I would like to end with the last poem in *A Hundred Doors*, 'Greenshank':

When I've left Carrigskeewaun for the last time,
I hope you discover something I've overlooked,

Greenshanks, say, two or three, elegantly probing
Where sand from the white strand and the burial mound
Blows in. How long will Corragaun remain a lake?
If I had to choose a bird call for reminding you,
The greenshank's estuarial fluting would do.

*A transcript of a lecture given in the John Hume Institute for Global Irish Studies,*
*University College Dublin, on 1 February 2010.*

# BIOGRAPHICAL NOTE

MICHAEL LONGLEY was born in Belfast in 1939 and educated at the Royal Belfast Academical Institution and Trinity College Dublin where he read Classics. He worked for the Arts Council of Northern Ireland for twenty years, initiating the programmes for Literature, the Traditional Arts (mainly Irish music) and Arts in Education. He has published ten collections of poetry including *Gorse Fires* (1991) which won the Whitbread Poetry Award, and *The Weather in Japan* (2000) which won the Hawthornden Prize, the T. S. Eliot Prize and the *Irish Times* Poetry Prize. His *Collected Poems* was published in 2006. His most recent collection is *The Stairwell* (2014). In 2001 he received the Queen's Gold Medal for Poetry, and in 2003 the Wilfred Owen Award. He was appointed a CBE in 2010. He is a Fellow of the Royal Society of Literature, a Fellow of the American Academy of Arts and Sciences, and a member of Aosdana. He was Ireland Professor of Poetry, 2007–10. He and his wife, the critic Edna Longley, live and work in Belfast. In 2015 he was made a Freeman of the City.

## A NOTE ON TEXTS

The poems by Michael Longley quoted in these lectures are drawn from the following collections:

*No Continuing City* (London: Macmillan, 1969)

*An Exploded View* (London: Gollancz, 1973)

*The Echo Gate* (London: Secker and Warburg, 1979)

*Gorse Fires* (London: Cape, 1991)

*After Ovid: New Metamorphoses*, edited by Michael Hofmann and James Lasdun (London: Faber and Faber, 1994)

*The Ghost Orchid* (London: Cape, 1995)

*Selected Poems* (London: Cape, 1998)

*The Weather in Japan* (London: Cape, 2000)

*Snow Water* (London: Cape, 2004)

*Collected Poems* (London: Cape, 2006)

*Wavelengths: Selected Translations* (London: Enitharmon Press, 2009)

*A Hundred Doors* (London: Cape, 2011)

*The Stairwell* (London: Cape, 2014)

Michael Longley has also published a memoir:

*Tuppenny Strung: Autobiographical Chapters* (Belfast: Lagan Press, 1994)

# ACKNOWLEDGEMENTS

*The author and publisher gratefully acknowledge the following for permission to reprint copyright material.*

Douglas Dunn: 'The Friendship of Young Poets', from *The Happier Life* (Faber and Faber, 1972). Reprinted by kind permission of Faber and Faber.

Paul Durcan: 'The Seal of Burrishoole', from *The Laughter of Mothers* (Harvill Press, 2007). Reprinted by kind permission of Rogers, Coleridge & White, 20 Powis Mews, London WII IJN.

Robert Graves: 'She Tells Her Love', from *Robert Graves: Complete Poems in One Volume* (Carcanet, 2000). Reprinted by kind permission of Carcanet Press.

Seamus Heaney: 'Cow in Calf', 'Personal Helicon', 'Synge on Aran', 'Lovers on Aran', from *Death of a Naturalist* (Faber and Faber, 1966), and six lines from *The Cure at Troy* (Faber and Faber, 1990). Reprinted by kind permission of Faber and Faber.

Patrick Kavanagh: 'Consider the Grass Growing', from *Collected Poems of Patrick Kavanagh*, edited by Antoinette Quinn (Allen Lane, 2004), reprinted by kind permission of the Trustees of the Estate of the late Katherine B. Kavanagh, through the Jonathan Williams Literary Agency.

Philip Larkin, 'Wedding-Wind', from *The Less Deceived* (Faber and Faber, 1955). Reprinted by kind permission of Faber and Faber.